beyond soccer

The World Stage

beyond soccer

The World Stage

Rich Daughtridge and John Stayskal

McDougal Publishing is a ministry of the The McDougal Foundation, Inc., a Maryland nonprofit corporation dedicated to spreading the Gospel of the Lord Jesus Christ to as many people as possible in the shortest time possible.

Published by:

McDougal Publishing
P.O. Box 3595
Hagerstown, MD 21742-3595

www.mcdougalpublishing.com

ISBN 1-58158-090-8 Trade Paper

Printed in the United States of America
For Worldwide Distribution

DVD

While preparing the second volume of *Beyond Soccer* this year, we also produced a professional DVD as a companion to the book. The DVD is FREE (shipping and handling - $3.95) to anyone who requests a copy via the Beyond Soccer web site. Please follow the special ordering instructions below. Available while supplies last.

The DVD features:

- Introduction: Soccer Ministry Highlights
- Interview and Highlights With Rich Daughtridge, produced by Breakaway Outreach
- (10) Player Tips
- (10) Coaching Tips
- Bloopers and Outtakes
- Soccer Ministry Index

To order, visit the following web address:
  www.beyondsoccer.org/dvd

Contents

About Beyond Soccer

Beyond Soccer is a sports ministry with a simple mission: *to offer a resource for Christian growth and discovery through the sport of soccer.* Our primary resource tools to-date are our devotional books *Beyond Soccer: The Ultimate Goal* and *Beyond Soccer: The World Stage*, both published by McDougal Publishing.

In less than two years, more than **twenty thousand copies** of *Beyond Soccer: The Ultimate Goal* have been printed and distributed to organizations and individuals around the United States, **quietly impacting the lives of people who love soccer.**

I'm amazed at how God has used this book in such a great way in such a short time. I'm just a little-known indoor soccer player. It's truly a testimony of what happens when we seek His will and focus on His purpose for our lives.—Rich Daughtridge

Beyond Soccer books are being used in conjunction with summer soccer camps, youth soccer tournaments, Bible studies, international soccer tours, team devotionals and ministry outreach opportunities.

In addition to traditional book sales through bookstores, web sites and direct sales, *Beyond Soccer* books are sold primarily to non-profit organizations at highly discounted rates. Once a year, during a campaign called Operation: Soccer Outreach, *Beyond Soccer* books are offered to organizations for only $2.00 per book. For more information on Operation: Soccer Outreach and how your organization can be involved, visit the special section near the end of the book.

For up-to-date news and information on Beyond Soccer, visit www.beyondsoccer.org.

Co-author: Rich Daughtridge

Rich Daughtridge is founder of Beyond Soccer, a ministry committed to offering resources for Christian growth through the sport of soccer.

Beyond Soccer has recently adopted an international perspective with the printing of *Beyond Soccer: The World Stage* and is actively pursuing the translation of this book into other languages. As the world's most popular sport, soccer offers a vehicle for spreading Christianity unlike any other. Beyond Soccer seeks to facilitate this mission through partnerships with other sports ministries, churches and missionary organizations.

In addition to Beyond Soccer, Rich also owns and manages High Rock Interactive, Inc., a marketing and web design company with offices in Hagerstown, Maryland, and Baltimore, Maryland.

Rich resides in Smithsburg, Maryland, with his wife, Susan, son, Reed, and daughter, Carter.

For up-to-date news and information on Beyond Soccer and a complete bio of Rich Daughtridge, visit www.beyondsoccer.org.

Co-author: John Stayskal

John Stayskal is founder and president of Ultimate Goal Ministries, a soccer missions organization. Founded in 1995, Ultimate Goal has taken hundreds of young soccer players around the world sharing the Good News of Jesus Christ through the common interest of soccer. Ultimate Goal has caught the attention of national ministries including Focus on the Family (*Brio, Breakaway and Life on the Edge*) and the Billy Graham Evangelistic Association (*Decision Today*, Passageway.org). Ultimate Goal's mission statement sums up their calling: "Making the soccer field our mission field." More information about Ultimate Goal can be found at www.ultimategoal.net.

John and his wife, Tracy, reside in Nashville, Tennessee. There they enjoy raising their sons, Luke, Paul and Timothy.

Boot Cleaning

John 13:3-5 (NKJ) *Jesus...rose from supper and laid aside His garments, took a towel and girded Himself. After that, He poured water into a basin and began to wash the disciples' feet, and to wipe them with the towel with which He was girded.*

Within most professional football organizations around the world, apprentices, oftentimes youth players from the club, will fulfill the duty of cleaning and polishing the boots of the players on the first team. At the higher levels, it's an unwritten perk of being a professional.

> *Part of leadership is servanthood.*

On this day, some of the players arrived at the stadium earlier than expected and began their routine to prepare for the big game ahead. One player glanced at his locker, shocked that his boots weren't laid out like they had been in all previous games. He fired off, "Where are my boots? How can they not have our boots ready?" A few others followed suit and began complaining. Thirty minutes passed by as more players made their way to the locker room, quickly introduced by the others to the harsh reality that "their boots were still not ready!" The buzz of annoyance continued amongst the players. "How could this happen? We're professionals!"

It had been a long week of practice figuring out why they were beaten the weekend before, and the coach had demanded a high level of concentration and focus from his players. Strategies were changed, individuals were told to "step up their game," and fitness level "was not going to be a reason they lose games, period!"

Ten minutes before the traditional walk out to the pitch to begin warm-ups, the coach burst through the door pushing a shopping cart full of freshly polished boots. His tie was shifted and loose, his white dress shirt was now wrinkled and stained with sweat, a rag lay draped on his shoulder. The players were shocked. "Guys, the boys who normally clean our boots were in an accident on the highway on the way to the stadium. They're fine, thank goodness, but they didn't make it in. Come get your shoes. OK, listen up; here's our game plan...."

Part of leadership is servanthood. Like Jesus, we must all remember the effectiveness of humbling ourselves for the greater purpose.

Jesus was the ultimate coach, and He led by example. On the day He washed the feet of His disciples, His team, He also knew it was the day He was supposed to die for the sins of all mankind. His act of humility and sacrifice was a symbol of love in the midst of chaos and tragedy. Under the banner of Christianity, His followers would duplicate that same example of love all around the world.

Fog Football

Proverbs 6:22 *When you walk about, they will **guide** you; when you sleep, they will watch over you; and when you awake, they will talk to you.*

In 1945 a very unusual thing happened in a game between Arsenal and Dynamo Moscow. A dense fog fell on the field, but the referee refused to call the game since the visiting team had traveled all the way from Moscow. The game was rapidly reduced to shambles. One Arsenal player was sent off for fighting, but he sneaked back on again in the fog. Dynamo substituted a player but never sent their other player off, and it was widely felt that they actually had up to fifteen players on the field at one time. Due to the fog, no one could actually see to count. The last strange incident happened when the Arsenal goalie became disorientated in the fog and ran into the goalpost and was knocked unconscious. He was replaced by a member of the crowd.

> *Have you ever felt like you were in a spiritual fog?*

Have you ever felt like you were in a spiritual fog, had a hard time seeing the path God has called you to walk in, or had a hard time knowing what was happening in life around you?

Only the sun clears up fog, and in the same way only the Son can clear spiritual fog.

Spiritual fog can be caused by sin, lack of a real relationship with Jesus Christ, or just by the things life throws at you.

Do you want to see clearly or

assist your friends in seeing clearly? Go to God in prayer and seek His Word. Ask Him to remove the fog making it hard for you to see. Follow His commands. Put your full trust in Him. Pilots can fly through fog, clouds or darkness by their instruments. You can live through the fog by putting your trust in a loving God and in His Word, the Bible.

Freedom Fan

The year was 1946, the location: Burnden Park, Bolton, England. It was a much-anticipated FA Cup game between the home team, Bolton Wanderers, and the visiting team, Stoke City. The game was a sixth-round tiebreaker in the quest for the coveted FA Cup.

Frank Jubb walked amongst the crowd this day with a half smile. He was enjoying his newly found freedom and the simple pleasure of watching a great football game once again. Seven weeks earlier, Mr. Jubb was serving in the Royal Artillery and had served during World War II, spending three years in a prisoner-of-war camp. He had now returned to Bolton to continue his employment with a building firm. After a troubled

Where do you want to spend eternity?

past, on this day the future seemed like a pleasant dream.

Ten minutes into the game, Stanley Matthews, the star of Stoke City, recalled later, "We had reason to feel confident, as we were having the best of the game. It then happened! There was a terrific roar from the crowd, and I glanced over my shoulder to see thousands of fans coming from the terracing behind the far goal onto the pitch." Estimates were later released that sixty-five thousand fans had occupied the stadium built for only forty-five thousand and, as a result, a section of the crush barriers had collapsed, causing a massive and violent stampede.

Frank Jubb died that day in the stadium tragedy. He had fought for freedom all those years and

survived as a prisoner of war.
Now, seven weeks later, he dies
a senseless death at a football
match, of all places.

The sobering reality is...we'll
all die someday. The question
then becomes: Where do you
want to spend eternity? We can
go through every week doing the
same thing every day, but where
is it getting us? What's the
result of the game?

Take a moment to reflect on
your life. If you haven't considered becoming a Christian,
consider it now. If you're in
need of recommitting your life to
Jesus Christ, do it now.

Go through life with a "half
smile," knowing there's a bigger
purpose than just what this life
has to offer.

Brazilian Youth

I Timothy 4:12 *Let no one look down on your youthfulness, but rather in speech, conduct, love, faith and purity, show yourself an example of those who believe.*

How old are you right now? What level of skill have you attained for your age?

Imagine being a young teenager and being good enough to play professionally. The United States has sixteen-year-old Freddie Adu. Brazil has thirteen-year-old Maicon Vinicius da Cruz, known as Nikao. The Dutch club PSV Eindhoven earned the right to sign him. There also was interest from FC Barcelona and Russia's CSKA Moscow. He will become eligible for transfer according to Brazilian law when he turns sixteen. Nikao is the second young player in Brazil to receive interest from European teams. A nine-year-old named Jean Carlos Chera had several teams, including Manchester United, contact his club in Brazil.

> *Regardless of how good you are on the football field, God wants you to make your greatest impression in the game of life.*

These players are so good at an early age that they are receiving interest from major clubs. They are looked up to by all the young (and old) players around them.

In a similar way, you should be looked up to by the young (and old) around you for your character, faith and witness. God's Word tells us to be examples in these areas. Regardless of how good you are on the football field, God wants you to make your greatest impression in the game of life. He wants others to be able to see Him in you, and be attracted by what they see. In your youth, who can you be an example to today? Whom can you introduce to Christ this week? Who needs to see God in you?

Ordinary Men

1 Samuel 16:7_"For God sees not as man sees, for man looks at the outward appearance, but the LORD looks at the heart."_

So how did your son get started playing football?

"Well, you know Ben. He wanted to play a sport. But he's too short for basketball, not fast enough for track, not strong enough to wrestle. I guess he fell into football because he's so…ordinary."

> _God chooses ordinary, average, everyday people to do His work._

That seems to sum it up for a lot of people, doesn't it? Look around at the next youth game you attend. What do you see? Boys, girls, short, tall, some faster, some slower, some slight, some husky. Just ordinary kids…until they hit the field. Suddenly, these average-looking kids meld into teams, working together, bursting with energy and enthusiasm. Football seems to have a way of bringing out that excitement and sense of purpose in its players.

God's team is a lot like that. God chooses ordinary, average, everyday people to do His work. Jesus' disciples were the fishermen, the tax collector, the doctor, the political activist. Together, they were used by God to change the world.

Whenever we feel beaten down by the ordinariness of life, we need to allow Jesus Himself to remind us that we are just where

He wants us to be. He looks beyond the externals to see our hearts. And if we ask Him, He will use those hearts to help change the world...for Him.

Saudi Slur

I Thessalonians 5:11 *Therefore encourage one another, and build up one another, just as you also are doing.*

After Hungary tied with Saudi Arabia in a game played in Turkey, the Hungarian prime minister, Ferenc Gyurcsany, made an inexcusable comment, saying that the Saudis had "very many terrorists" on their team. He was quoted as saying, "I think that there were very many terrorists also among the Saudi football players, and our sons fought with death-defying bravery against these terrorists, so a draw away from home is a fantastic result."

He later apologized, saying it was just a joke, but regardless, it should never have been said.

All too often we say things,

> *Scripture tells us to encourage one another.*

hopefully not this drastic, that offend, hurt, cut down, belittle and criticize people. Sometimes we say those things in a joking manner, and other times they come out of frustration and anger.

The negative, discouraging, mean things we say about people often drive them further into discouragement and pain, and many times further from God.

Scripture tells us to encourage one another. Life is tough enough. Everyone around us has things they are dealing with personally. Some people are looking hard for life's answers. Others are searching for God. Why risk hurting people by saying or doing anything that would discourage them further? We must look around us and be determined to encourage one another. Why not ask God today to show you who you can encourage and lift up. You never know; they might really need it and your encouragement might be a life-changing thing for them.

The Stadium of Your Life

2 Corinthians 5:1 (NKJ) *For we know that if our earthly house, this tent, is destroyed, we have a building from God, a house not made with hands, eternal in the heavens.*

The Maracana Stadium in Rio de Janeiro, Brazil, is the world's largest football stadium, with a capacity of 180,000. It was reported that 199,854 spectators were squeezed in to watch the 1950 World Cup final between Brazil and Uruguay. Uruguay won that game 2-1.

The Maracana Stadium, taking its name from the small river that flows by the structure, is where Pele scored his one thousandth goal. It's also home to the renowned football club Flamingo.

Although this massive structure continues to dominate the

Just like the small river that continually flows by the Maracana each day, life flows by all of us.

cityscape of Rio de Janeiro, its glory days are long gone unless extravagant amounts of money are spent to restore many of the sections deemed unsafe and unusable. In 1998, major renovations were made under the authority of FIFA, the world governing body of football, and the capacity is now set at only 70,000.

In less than fifty years, a stadium such as this, in all its glory and history, is now beginning to crumble. Think of all the energy, time and money it took to build it. Now what's left?

In life we often do the same

thing. Our focus is on building our careers, making money, succeeding in business. One day, perhaps at the age of fifty, when you look back to see what you've built, will it be something that's only material? Or will it be something with eternal value?

Just like the small river that continually flows by the Maracana each day, life flows by all of us. Take time to step back and look at your life. Consider your stadium.

A Huge Mistake

Romans 6:23 *For the wages of sin is death, but the free gift of God is eternal life in Christ Jesus our Lord.*

Bobby Robson, manager of Newcastle, saw Jason Euell playing for Wimbledon and was impressed to the point of being interested in pursuing him. Not remembering his name, Bobby asked his scout to inquire about the "young black lad" playing the forward position for England's under-21 team.

In the meantime, England moved another young black player, Carl Cort, to the forward position and moved Jason into the midfield.

The scout asked Bobby if he wanted to put a bid in for Carl, believing him to be the young black lad Bobby had inquired about. Bobby said yes and set the offer at 7.5 million pounds.

Jason was by far a more talented player than Carl, and unquestionably worth the 7.5 million pounds Bobby was willing to pay, while Carl's value was nowhere near that amount. So upon receiving the offer, Wimbledon couldn't sign fast enough.

> *Sin is what separates us from a relationship with God.*

Soon Bobby realized he had made a huge mistake and purchased the wrong player.

Have you ever made a huge mistake? How about a small one? Honestly, we all do, every day. Some mistakes affect others; some only affect us and no one ever knows about them. Scripture calls our mistakes sin. Sin is what separates us from a relationship with God.

Thankfully, we can all turn to Jesus to forgive us of the mis-takes we make that separate us from God. His free gift of forgiveness is for everyone.

Don't allow any more time to pass before correcting your mistakes.

The Big Picture

Jeremiah 29:11 *"For I know the plans that I have for you,"*
declares the LORD, "plans for welfare and not for calamity to give
you a future and a hope."

1998 was the first time in twenty years that Iran had qualified for the World Cup. It was a time of strained relations with the United States, as the two countries had been bitter enemies since Ayatollah Ruhollah Khomeini's rise to power in 1979. Ironically, when the teams were matched by random draw, Iran was slated to play the U.S.

As the game approached, U.S. President Clinton issued statements of hope that the game could lead to an improvement in relations between the two countries. Just before the match, starting players for each team exchanged gifts as a token of peace and sportsmanship.

Although favored to win easily, U.S. players made several mistakes, allowing Iran to land a 2-0 victory. Yet there was more to that contest than an Iranian football triumph. The teams showed they could face each other on the field and play a competitive game, but in peace.

> *Our focus is to be on living a life of purpose.*

We, too, are to look at the big picture. Our emphasis is not to be on external success or on making money. Our focus is to be on living a life of purpose. When we seek God's purpose for our lives, we can be assured that we will find it. And as we live at peace with our Creator, we can show others a way of hope as well.

Football Quiz

Luke 10:25 *A certain lawyer stood up and put Him to the test, saying, "Teacher, what shall I do to inherit eternal life?"*

How well do you know the game of football? Test yourself with these questions.

1. What is the name by which Edson Arantes do Nascimiento is best known?

2. In what country does football have its roots?

3. What is the only country to appear in every World Cup since 1950?

4. How many miles does the average football player run in a typical game?

5. Where is the next World Cup to be hosted?

How well do you think you answered these questions? Check your answers on the next page.

A lawyer in the Bible tried to test Jesus on the question of eternal life.

The biggest test of our life comes when our time on this earth ends and we are asked what we did with the person of Jesus? There is only one right answer. Our answer and how we lived our life will determine our eternal destiny. If we can answer that He was our Savior and Lord and we lived our life for Him, then we receive eternal life with God. Eternal life with God is what He desires for each of us.

Eternal life with God is what He desires for each of us.

Fortunately, God sent Jesus to show us the way to Himself and prepare us for the biggest quiz of our lives. We've all been given the answer. It's up to us to choose to live our lives for Jesus Christ.

1. Pele

2. England

3. Brazil

4. Between 6 and 7

5. Germany (2006)

Future and Hope

Jeremiah 29:11-13 (NLT) *"For I know the plans I have for you,"
says the LORD. "They are plans for good and not for disaster, to give
you a future and a hope. In those days when you pray, I will listen. If
you look for me in earnest, you will find me when you seek me."*

I was in Jamaica as a guest
coach working with players
in the final stages of
training before their season
started. My stay was almost up
and we had only one more
exhibition match to
play in Kingston.
The match had just
gotten under way
when those of us on
the sideline and on
the field heard a horrendously
loud crash. Although several
blocks away from the field, the
crash sounded like it was close
by. Thoughts that ran through
my mind told me that no one
could have survived. And on the
side line the coaching staff and
the reserve players all agreed
with what my mind was experi-

> *God's got a special
> plan for you and
> it's a great one.*

encing. No one said anything at
halftime. Many were shocked
and simply glad that they were
alive and safe as the crash rang
out death.

A few moments after the match
had ended we
noticed the car on
the bed of a tow
truck. It was de-
stroyed. It didn't
look like a car anymore. I could
only think, *What a disaster!*

Being the guest coach, I was
asked to share a few closing
words before I left to catch a
plane. A few parting words?
What could I say after such a
crash? I managed to share a few
coaching points and a few words
of appreciation, but my mind

was still on the life that was lost in the crash. It was a full two weeks of coaching and I had been able to impact players not only in football, but also spiritually. With all the team and coaching staff gathered around, one guy asked if the team would ever see me again. I said, "Some will and some will not. It's like this, men: This morning the person in the car crash never knew what disaster they would face today. They didn't know it would be the last day of their life on this earth. You guys, God's got a special plan for you and it's a great one. It's beyond football. It's His special design for you and your choice. Those who follow Him here on this earth will one day be with Him in Heaven. That's a great promise for you from God. Don't choose a road that will be your disaster and your ending. You just never know when your time is up. I trust you'll be ready to look for God's Son as your Savior, because if this is the prayer of your heart, I'll see you again for sure one day. God bless."

What Are You Worth?

Matthew 6:26 (NIV) *"Look at the birds of the air; they do not sow or reap or store away in barns, and yet your heavenly Father feeds them. Are you not much more valuable than they?"*

In one of the most anticipated deals ever, David Beckham was sold from Manchester United to Real Madrid for forty-one million dollars. Real Madrid shirts bearing his name and his new number 23 were sold out in Madrid on the day his transfer was completed, and his new club was expected to receive $748,000 for their sale. At the time of the announcement of his transfer to Real Madrid, Beckham and his wife were on a week-long tour of the Far East promoting beauty products, chocolate, motor oil and mobile phones, which would earn them more than the entire first year of his Real Madrid contract.

> *Show others their worth by how you treat them.*

Imagine being worth the payment of forty-one million dollars for your talent, or your "image" earning hundreds of thousands of dollars in shirt sales.

I have good news for you. You are worth far more than forty-one million dollars. Jesus Christ paid much more than money to show you how much He values you. You were worth every drop of blood He shed on the cross in giving His life for you. You were so valuable to Him that He gave His very life, suffering terrible beatings, mockings and being nailed to a cross for YOU!

All the people you know, your teammates, neighbors and friends, are worth the same amount to Jesus Christ. You are valuable to Him. We need to value each other in the same way. Show others their worth by how you treat them. Demonstrate to your non-Christian friends how much Jesus Christ values them by taking time today to share Jesus in practical ways. You were worth it and they are worth it.

The Source of Victory

Proverbs 21:31 (MSG) *Do your best, prepare for the worst—then trust GOD to bring victory.*

In their first-ever World Cup appearance, in 2002, Senegal was the surprise sensation. They not only made the finals, but they were also the only African team to make it past the group stage. They courageously lost in extra time to Turkey 1-0 in the quarterfinals.

However, their road to the quarterfinals was not always a smooth one. The reigning king of global football, Pele, remarked before the tournament, "Senegal is the weakest team in the tournament." They also had to fight the stigma of being in their first-ever World Cup. It was not an easy road.

But they persevered through the challenges and in the end it paid off. If not for all of the hard work, the disappointments along the way and the intense preparation, they would not have helped an entire continent hope for the impossible.

> *Trust Him to guide you to victory today.*

How is your climb toward the top? You no doubt have had or will have setbacks. The Bible tells us that we must train and must do our best but that ultimately, victory comes from God. In the midst of your training and striving toward your mark of excellence, never forget that in the end, it is God who brings you victory. Trust Him to guide you to victory today.

The World's Stage

Matthew 5:16 *"Let your light shine before men in such a way that they may see your good works, and glorify your Father who is in heaven."*

When Asia was hit with a devastating tsunami, the world came to the aid of those people. Millions of dollars were donated, along with medical supplies, clothing and food. Rescue workers and medical personnel went to Asia to give of their time and expertise. This disaster and the world's response were on the world stage. Everyone was watching the events unfold and everyone seemed to participate in one way or another, including through prayer.

World football players even got involved to raise three million dollars for tsunami relief.

Players like Ronaldo, Zinedine Zidane, Samuel Eto'o, Henry Camara and Iker Casillas came together to play in an all-star benefit game.

The popularity of football and the opportunity to help with a great need came together.

> *Help meet a great need, people's need for a savior.*

On a much smaller scale, but no less important, is the opportunity for you to take the popularity of football to help meet a great need, people's need for a savior, Jesus Christ.

Because of the common interest of football, and the ability to break through cultural barriers, you have the opportunity to have an impact on the world stage, right at home.

Let me encourage you to use your gifts in football to reach out and build relationships with those around you who might only be reached through the common interest of football.

Some will never enter a church, for whatever reason, but will pass a ball around with you, join a tournament, enter a league or attend a camp/clinic. Your good works on a small scale are just as important as the larger works visible to everyone.

Painfully Let Down

Proverbs 3:5-6 (NKJ) *Trust in the LORD with all your heart, and lean not on your own understanding; in all your ways acknowledge Him, and He shall direct your paths.*

Have you ever been let down by the people you trusted most? Ever felt the crushing pain of despair when friends, family, coworkers and teammates failed to support you in your time of greatest need? Steve Morrow certainly has, and he bears the scars to prove it! Having scored the goal that crowned Arsenal as the 1993 League Champions of England, he was tossed high into the air by his jubilant and grateful teammates. Unfortunately for Steve, the same people who sent him skyward in their moment of elation were the same ones who failed to catch him on his descent. They lifted him up, only to let him down (literally), and Steve found himself being carried off the field on a stretcher with a broken arm and with an oxygen mask on his face.

> *When others fall short, Jesus Christ stands tall.*

Steve Morrow's story gives us a perfect illustration of just how risky it is to put our trust completely in people. We are often disappointed by their lack of integrity or their inability to empathize with our current situation. They oppose us without justification and they damage our reputation. They fail in their commitments and in their responsibilities. In short, they demonstrate the very same human frailties that we ourselves exhibit, yet condemn in others.

Thankfully, we have a Savior who can be trusted at all times and in all circumstances. When others fall short, Jesus Christ stands tall, and when our life is ravaged by the attitudes and actions of those around us, Jesus calms our storm and reminds us that He'll never leave us nor forsake us.

Are you wounded today because of public opinion or strained relationships? Like Steve Morrow, you've been let down and have suffered through no fault of your own. Jesus Christ is ready and waiting to pick you up, to embrace you and to prove Himself a true and trusted friend!

Changing Allegiances

Acts 26:17-18 (NIV) *"I am sending you to them to open their eyes and turn them from darkness to light, and from the power of Satan to God, so that they may receive forgiveness of sins and a place among those who are sanctified by faith in me."*

Recently, FIFA created a rule change that would allow players to switch their national allegiance, allowing them to start a new career after having previously represented another country at the junior level. The rule change has allowed such players as former England under-21 captain Ben Thatcher to become a Welsh international and Tim Cahill of Everton to represent Australia, his native land. As of this writing, twenty countries, including Ireland, Wales, Australia, Venezuela and several African countries, have benefited from this rule change.

> *To whom is your allegiance pledged?*

In the book of Acts in the Bible, Jesus sent out the disciples to share with people the opportunity they had to change their spiritual allegiances, from darkness to light and from the power of Satan to God, so that they would receive forgiveness of sins.

What an opportunity for people to come "home," to return to their Maker, to serve the true and living God. Are you in for a "career" change? Have you been serving the wrong person or thing? Now is the time to switch allegiances.

Through a rule change by FIFA, players are able to change their national allegiances. Because of what Jesus did on the cross, we can change allegiances from a life of sin, desperation and hopelessness to a life of joy, peace and forgiveness in Christ.

To whom is your allegiance pledged? Is it to Christ or to someone else? If it is not to Christ, you can make the decision today to change your allegiance to Him and begin playing for your new team.

Anger Management

Proverbs 29:11 (NIV) *A fool gives full vent to his anger, but a wise man keeps himself under control.*

A football advertisement once quipped, "1966 was a great year for English football—Eric Cantona was born!" Hailed as a football genius for his sublime skill, wonderful vision and outstanding goals, Cantona was regarded by many as the most influential football player in England during the 1990s. He was idolized at Manchester United and worshiped as "Eric the King." In a total of 181 appearances for United, Cantona scored a remarkable 80 goals, won the coveted FA Cup twice and the Premier League four times. In 1994, Cantona earned the recognition of his fellow professionals by winning the Players' Football Association (PFA) Player of the Year award, and in 1996 he was voted Footballer of the Year by the Football Writers' Association. Cantona went on to captain his country (France), scoring nineteen goals in forty-five appearances between 1987 and 1994. At age thirty, after winning the Premiership title in 1997, Eric Cantona announced his retirement from professional football, leaving the game in his magnificent prime, preferring to be remembered as a winner rather than an aging player past his best.

> *Choose wisdom... for your benefit and the benefit of others!*

And yet memories of Eric Cantona are rarely restricted to the football field alone. Few will ever forget the infamous "kung fu kick" in January 1995 when the volatile Frenchman leapt into the crowd, aiming a two-footed lunge at a Crystal Palace supporter who reportedly shouted racial insults and threw missiles at the red-carded Cantona as he left the field. The United star was fined twenty thousand pounds (U.K.), he was stripped of his captaincy of the French National team, and he lost his place in the side. He also received a worldwide ban from football for nine months and was sentenced to two weeks in prison (later reduced to 120 hours of community service).

Less well known, but no less indicative of a serious character flaw, Cantona insulted the French National team manager on television in 1988 and was banned from the National side for a year. In addition, while playing for Nîmes before joining United, he threw the ball at a

referee and was banned for three matches. In the disciplinary hearing that followed, Cantona confronted three members of the French FA and shouted "idiot" in each of their faces, leading to another ban, this time for two months.

Without doubt, Eric Cantona's retirement from the game left a void which has perhaps never been filled. And yet his claim to greatness has been marred by acts of insolence, violence, disrespect and anger. His rebellious nature and inability to control his tongue and his temper, have taken the gloss off a glittering and memorable playing career. In fact, while the football world applauds Cantona's achievements and is inspired by his remarkable talent, the Scriptures call him a "fool" for his lack of self-control during times of frustration, anger and insult. A harsh commentary indeed on a man who gave so much to the game of football but who lacked wisdom to temper his reaction to difficult circumstances.

Life presents many challenges to the Christian, not least of which is the call to Christ-likeness during times of strife and conflict. We are to remain self-controlled and demonstrate God's wisdom in handling people who come against us or who disagree with our view-point. We are not to match violence with violence, and we should learn to "turn the other cheek" when confronted with a verbal volley. Tempting though it is to fight back, we Christians are to ask God for His strength to see us through those moments when the easy way is to "get even" rather than rise above the oppressor.

What is God's estimation of you? Are you considered wise in your reactions to the trials of life, or foolish as you vent your anger just like Eric Cantona. Choose wisdom...for your benefit and the benefit of others!

El Salvador Football School

Psalm 1:1-3 *How blessed is the man who does not walk in the counsel of the wicked, nor stand in the path of sinners, nor sit in the seat of scoffers! But his delight is in the law of the LORD, and in His law he meditates day and night. And he will be like a tree firmly planted by streams of water, which yields its fruit in its season, and its leaf does not wither; and in whatever he does, he prospers.*

Not known for its football success, the country of El Salvador has announced its plan to start a football academy with two hundred junior players. Their goal is to help their county become a World Cup contender again.

In attempting to qualify for the 2006 World Cup, El Salvador won only one of six games in the CONCACAF semifinal round. They failed to score a goal in their last five.

El Salvador hopes to produce up to forty potential professional-level players each year.

Sometimes, constant dedication and focus are needed to produce what we desire.

The natural result of spending time in God's Word is that we will bear fruit.

Do you desire to grow as a Christian? Would you like your walk with God to be closer? Do you want God to use you in a greater way?

Psalm 1 says that the man is blessed who delights in God's law and meditates on it day and night. The results for any of us in doing this are the following: We will be like trees firmly planted near streams of water, bearing fruit, not dying and prospering in all we do.

The natural result of spending time in God's Word, thinking on it and applying it to our lives is that we will bear fruit, we'll be productive Christians, and God will use us in great ways beyond our expectations.

Just as the country of El Salvador is focusing on their training of players to improve their World Cup chances, in a similar way, we can focus on our spiritual lives to become more effective Christians.

The International Language

Philippians 4:7 (KJV) *And the peace of God, which passeth all understanding, shall keep your hearts and minds through Christ Jesus.*

Football has often been called "the international language," for it's a sport that crosses political, social and economic lines, breaking down barriers of race, geography and even the tragedies of world history. Countries forget about fighting for a moment. Young boys sit mesmerized, dreaming of a chance to wear that jersey. Fanatics dance and sing, echoing chants throughout the stadium. Everyone waits in utter anticipation for that decisive goal. Stadiums burst out in random applause as players showcase their skill, and the corner *barrio* becomes the scene of chatter and a thousand opinions. Small towns and major cities alike appear deserted as businesses unapologetically flip their signs to "closed."

> *Becoming a Christian is not reserved for certain nationalities or people with certain backgrounds; it's an international opportunity.*

Christianity has a similar effect on the world. Lonely, empty hearts wander through life, never realizing what the future could be like with Jesus Christ as their friend and savior. Becoming a Christian is not reserved for certain nationalities or people with certain backgrounds; it's an international opportunity. As in football, there are ups and downs and victories and defeats in the game of life, but as a Christian you have the opportunity to live that life with a peace that passes all understanding.

The Heart of a Footballer

Proverbs 27:19 (NKJ) *As in water face reflects face, so a man's heart reveals the man.*

The game of football is like no other when it comes to passion, the passion exemplified by the players after scoring a goal or by the colorful fans who chant and sing hours before the game.

This passion comes from the heart.

At Camp Nou, the world-renowned stadium in Barcelona, Spain, Rivaldo scores a brilliant diving header and quickly jumps to his feet and celebrates against a backdrop of Barcelona blue. At the same time, nine thousand miles west across the Atlantic Ocean in Guadalajara, Mexico, a thirteen-year-old boy sprints to the sideline being chased by his teammates after scoring the game-winning goal for his school team. The reaction to these events, so different in scale, is the same in each player's heart, the same heart where God stands knocking to

> *The reaction to these events, so different in scale, is the same in each player's heart.*

come in. In Revelation 3:20, Jesus says, *"Behold, I stand at the door and knock; if anyone hears My voice and opens the door, I will come in to him, and will dine with him, and he with Me."*

Peru's Coach

2 Timothy 3:16 *All Scripture is inspired by God and profitable for teaching, for reproof, for correction, for training in righteousness.*

Peruvian club Cienciano recently brought back Uruguayan coach Daniel Jurado. Jurado, who coached Cienciano in 2001-2002, is said to have planted the seeds of their success during that time, which led them to win their only international trophy, the Copa Sudamericana, in 2003.

> *In our Christian walk, we too need a coach, someone to lead us, and spur us on to victory.*

All teams want to have the right coach, the one who can lead them to victory, bring the right players together, and create success.

Cienciano hired the coach they felt would bring them that success; after all, many felt he gave them what they needed to win their first international trophy.

In our Christian walk, we too need a coach, someone to lead us, and spur us on to victory. For us as Christians, that coach is God, and the playbook is the Bible. It contains everything we need for spiritual training and instruction in righteousness. God cares for and loves us and wants to bring us to victory in our lives.

Some reading this may have never made God the coach of your life. Others, like this Peurvian club who brought back a coach from the past, might have had God as your coach for a while, but then removed Him from your life. In both cases, you need God to be your coach: Either you need to invite Him into your life for the first time or you need to bring Him back into your life.

Just humbly talk to Him and ask Him to be your coach, to lead and guide you, to train and instruct you. Then get around others who have also made this decision, so that you can grow together.

Old Lion

Jeremiah 29:11 (KJV) *For I know the thoughts that I think toward you, saith the LORD, thoughts of peace, and not of evil, to give you an expected end.*

Roger Milla loved football. As his technique developed, he became known for his skill, and he signed for his first club at the age of thirteen. How could the big time be far away?

Yet his career never really took off. Finally, in 1978, Roger was part of Cameroon's winning team at the World Cup finals. His career ended soon afterward. Or so he thought.

Then he received a phone call from the president of his country, requesting his help. Roger came out of retirement, at the age of thirty-eight. His career was reignited. He led Cameroon to the FIFA World Cup quarter-finals—unprecedented for an African team. Roger holds many records in his sport; he has become a humanitarian and a national hero.

> *God has a purpose for you.*

Throughout the years of discouragement, Roger might not have seen what God had in mind for his life. Others might have looked on him as something of a failure—or at least not much of a success. It wasn't until he was called out of retirement at age thirty-eight that he made his mark on the game. Yet God had a plan for him from the beginning...as He does for you. No matter what your life may look like right now, know that God has a purpose for you. You can place your trust in Him.

The Hand of God

Deuteronomy 5:15 *"And you shall remember that you were a slave in the land of Egypt, and the LORD your God brought you out of there by a mighty hand and by an outstretched arm; therefore the LORD your God commanded you to observe the sabbath day."*

In the 1986 World Cup, Diego Maradona of Argentina electrified the world with his talent, quickness and goal-scoring ability. At the age of only seventeen, he scored more goals than anyone else and ultimately led Argentina to a World Cup championship. In the third game of the tournament, Argentina faced England, another powerhouse team expected to do well that year. As a cross came in from the left side in the ninety-eighth minute, Maradona jumped to meet the ball just past the outstretched arms of Peter Shilton, England's world-renowned goalkeeper. In a split second, Maradona, realizing the ball was out of reach, quickly raised his right arm and redirected the ball into the net with his fist. The referees, shielded from the play, all missed it and the goal stood as the Argentina players smothered Maradona in celebration. Photographs would later confirm the hand ball, and the goal became know as "the hand of God."

> *When we seek God, our lives are blessed.*

Although this sports highlight is not biblical in nature, we can certainly find parallels in our Christian walk. How many times have we tried to go it on our own? Or maybe some of you may have always relied on yourself, and never felt the need to rely on God. When we seek God, our lives are blessed. In the study guide *Experiencing God: Knowing and Doing the Will of God,* by Henry T. Blackaby and Claude V. King, they outline four places to look for God's will and perfect plan for our lives: the Bible, prayer, circumstances and the church. These four, when considered together, help us understand God's will and perfect plan for our lives. As you begin to follow Him and make Him a part of every decision in your life, you will one day look back in amazement at how the hand of God led you to where you are today.

Fight the Good Fight

1 Timothy 6:12 (NIV) *Fight the good fight of the faith.*

Unfortunately, all too often we read headlines such as "At Least 15 Dead in Syrian Football Riots" or "Football Hooliganism in Europe." The passions and anger of fans get out of control and fights or riots break out, often with deadly consequences.

These fights are not good. They are based in anger, jealousy and bitterness. Some unfold due to unresolved issues from heated rivalries between teams or even between countries.

Paul, in the book of 1Timothy in the Bible, encourages his son in the faith to fight the good fight of the faith. He wasn't referring to a physical fight, but to a fight for the faith, a battle to endure in his faith.

Scripture uses the words *fight*, *armor* and *battle* to symbolize the spiritual conflict between good (God) and evil (Satan).

The bottom line is that there is a battle going on for our souls. God's desire is for us to live for Him, while Satan only desires to destroy our lives.

God's desire is for us to live for Him.

You need to fight to stay spiritually pure. Don't just ease through life; prepare yourself for battle. How? Make sure you pray and read God's Word every day. Memorize and meditate on scripture. Become accountable to others through a small group or close friends. Fellowship with other Christians who will help and encourage you in your walk with Christ. Seek help from friends and God when tempted. These are all things you can do to help protect yourself in the battle for your soul.

Football of Hope

Ephesians 2:10 (KJV) *For we are his workmanship, created in Christ Jesus unto good works, which God hath before ordained that we should walk in them.*

December 26, 2004, was a day of tragedy. More than two hundred thousand people lost their lives in the deadly Indian Ocean tsunami. Many were left without loved ones, without homes, without jobs. Victims were at risk for exposure and disease. Around the world, people mourned...and tried to help.

> We were created with a larger purpose than merely to live for ourselves.

February 15, 2005, was a day of victory. That day the world's top footballers came together to raise money for the victims of the tsunami tragedy. The "Football of Hope" benefit match brought stars from various teams and countries together for a game that fans would dream of. **Ronaldo, Henry, Beckham, Zidane**...the world's greatest came together, not to further their careers or to earn money for themselves, but to freely give of their time and effort to raise nearly ten million dollars for the Tsunami Solidarity Fund.

Didn't these players have anything better to do with their time and talents? Apparently they didn't think so. They were looking at a greater purpose than themselves, a goal that went well beyond football. We each have a purpose that goes beyond our jobs or our pastimes. We were created with a larger purpose than merely to live for ourselves. Allow the Lord to show you His purpose for you. Let Him set the goal; then run for it with all you have.

Peace Cup

Romans 12:18 *If possible, so far as it depends on you, be at peace with all men.*

There is something about the game of football that makes it more than just another sport. Football seems to bring people together in a way other games don't. Take the Peace Cup, for instance.

Every other year, a tournament is held that attracts clubs and champions from different nations. Players come from the Netherlands and Korea, the United States, Argentina and France, among other nations. They come together, not to promote themselves, their nations or their teams, but to promote peace. World peace through football? That's the idea.

> *As you live each day, seek peace with those around you.*

"The objective of the tournament is to present and spread the vision of peace and culture in the world through football," Peace Cup chairman Rev. Chung Hwan Kwak has said. The profits from the games are used to nurture the hopes and dreams of young people in Third World countries.

You might not be playing for the Peace Cup this year. But according to the Scriptures, your actions are just as significant. As you live each day, seek peace with those around you. Walk in the peace that only Christ can bring, and you will find yourself sharing that peace with others.

Lost in Switzerland

Mark 8:36 *"For what does it profit a man to gain the whole world, and forfeit his soul?"*

Did you hear what happened to Paolo Diogo? While celebrating a goal for his Swiss team, Paolo Diogo, a Portuguese player, caught his wedding ring on a fence, and when he jumped down, ripped off the top of his finger. He must have been extremely excited, because before realizing what had happened, the referee cited Paolo for excessive celebration. Later Paolo went on to tell how he realized what had happened when his hand began to hurt "tremendously." The finger was found, but doctors were unable to reattach it and suggested amputation for the rest of the finger. Paolo took it all in stride, saying, "So I have to live with one less finger."

Are you losing your soul, or are you making your relationship with God most important?

OK, so losing a finger probably isn't that big of a deal (I say that will all my fingers intact). But what about losing your soul? The Bible makes it clear that gaining the world but losing your soul is not a place we want to find ourselves. Gaining material goods, status and all the things the world says we should have to be important or successful, while ignoring the most important thing in our lives, a relationship with God, is not worth it. When we die, we won't be able to take anything with us. Only our soul (spirit) will live on. Is it really worth losing your soul for temporary status, material goods or worldly success? I don't think so.

Examine your life today. Are you losing your soul, or are you making your relationship with God most important?

German Football Scandal

Hebrews 13:5 *"I will never desert you, nor will I ever forsake you."*

As I write, preparations for the 2006 World Cup in Germany are taking place as a serious scandal is developing, with referees and players under investigation for fixing matches for money. This is Germany's worst football scandal in over thirty years and it has damaged the country's football institution.

Regardless of this or other football scandals, will it really affect those of us who love the game? Millions of people around the world will continue to play the world's greatest sport. We won't stop playing or loving the game because a few have cheated.

The church and Christianity also have their fair share of scandal. But unlike the game of football, people use the scandals within the church as an excuse to quit attending or to quit growing in their faith. Others, who are not yet believers, use the scandals as an excuse to avoid any interest in the church or in Christianity, labeling all who associate with the church as hypocrites.

Let your faith have its foundation in your relationship with God.

If you are in that place, or ever find yourself there, please remember that people will fail you. Let your faith have its foundation in your relationship with God, not in man, so that when scandals come, your faith will be rooted and grounded in Him, and because of your love for God, you will move on, continually growing in your faith. We keep playing football because we love it, regardless of the scandals. In the same way, keep your faith in God strong because of your love for Him, regardless of the scandals.

Winning in the Second Half

by Richard A. Daughtridge, Pastor/Soccer Coach

It's halftime. The players are huddled around, totally disappointed with the first half. The score is 4-0, though not in our favor. "We're making mistake after mistake." The sad eyes that gazed at me, the coach, that day said one thing: defeat. Everyone on the team was reliving their failures, mentally picturing a slow-motion replay of every mistake. As a coach, I wanted to turn back time, rewind the clock and erase the tapes that they were now playing in their minds. Every coach has been there.

Sound familiar?

Life also offers a mixture of wins and losses, but we must win the most important game, the game of life. The game's prize: eternal life and a personal relationship with God.

I remember my halftime speech that day.

"The first half belongs to the coach. I take full responsibility for the score. Let me take the blame and you focus on what you will do in the second half. The other team is known for its fast speed of play. Let's slow them down! We need to possess the ball more and move the ball up the field. You must win the individual battles. Pass the ball only when you must, and dribble until pressured. Once pressured, I want that player to have options to pass to open players. The first half was mine. This second half belongs to you. Now get out there and win!"

We won that game. I don't think that it was due to those tactics totally, but rather because they were able to erase the failure so that they could see the hope. After the game, one father asked his daughter what the coach said at halftime. She answered, "The coach became guilty for the first half."

As I reflect, it reminds me of the story of how God loved man so much that He erased his guilt and defeat by taking the guilt and punishment on Himself. He died on a cross for you. God offers you an empty slate, forgiveness and a second chance in which He will become your personal coach in all you do. While we were yet sinners, Christ died for us. He accepted the guilt and penalty for all of our wrong, and He offers a new playbook for life.

We must all come to the realization that we will have a final whistle in the game of life. How do we make sure we're on that winning team?

If you haven't yet accepted God's forgiveness, take a moment alone and just say this simple prayer:

God, I accept Your Son, Jesus Christ, as my Savior. Forgive me for my past and help me to live for You in the future. I give You my life and want to live for You. In Christ's name I pray. Amen.

Now don't stop there. This is only the beginning. He gave us a plan to start us off in the second half. Here are a few kickoff principles and scriptures to begin your second half.

· **Be convinced.** Believe that Jesus Christ is God Almighty, Creator of the universe, who came in the form of man and accepted the penalty of death on behalf of mankind, offering eternal life to all who believe and accept salvation though Him.

John 3:16-17 (NIV) *"For God so loved the world that he gave his one and only Son, that whoever believes in him shall not perish but have eternal life. For God did not send his Son into the world to condemn the world, but to save the world through him."*

- **Be forgiven.** Repent of your wrong. In a simple prayer, ask your newfound Savior and friend for His help in becoming the person that He desires for you to become. He will forgive and erase your past.

Mark 1:15 (NIV) *"The time has come," he said. "The kingdom of God is near. Repent and believe the good news!"*

- **Be proclaiming.** Confess to others about your newfound relationship with Jesus Christ.

Romans 10:9-10 (NIV) *That if you confess with your mouth, "Jesus is Lord," and believe in your heart that God raised him from the dead, you will be saved. For it is with your heart that you believe and are justified, and it is with your mouth that you confess and are saved."*

- **Be baptized.** As commanded in the Bible, be baptized in obedience to His Word and to identify with His Church.

Acts 2:38 (NIV) *"Repent and be baptized, every one of you, in the name of Jesus Christ for the forgiveness of your sins. And you will receive the gift of the Holy Spirit."*

- **Be discipled.** Find a church to attend and be faithful to study, worship and connect with friends in the faith.

Matthew 28:19-20 (NIV) *"Therefore go and make disciples of all nations, baptizing them in the name of the Father and of the Son and of the Holy Spirit, and teaching them to obey everything I have commanded you. And surely I am with you always, to the very end of the age."*

DVD

While preparing the volume of *Beyond Soccer* this year, we also produced a professional DVD as a companion to the book. The DVD is FREE (shipping and handling - $3.95) to anyone who requests a copy via the Beyond Soccer web site. Please follow the special ordering instructions below. Available while supplies last.

The DVD features:

- Introduction: Soccer Ministry Highlights
- Interview and Highlights With Rich Daughtridge, produced by Breakaway Outreach
- (10) Player Tips
- (10) Coaching Tips
- Bloopers and Outtakes
- Soccer Ministry Index

To order, visit the following web address:
www.beyondsoccer.org/dvd

Operation: Soccer Outreach

Each year, during a campaign called Operation: Soccer Outreach, we offer copies of *Beyond Soccer* to organizations and individuals for only $2.00 each. In cooperation with McDougal Publishing, this promotion allows ministries around the world to use the books as a ministry outreach tool. In addition, all organizations who participate in Operation: Soccer Outreach are added to the "Partners" area on our web site. In 2005, they were featured on the DVD in a special section.

Some examples of uses for *Beyond Soccer* from years past include:

- **Soccer Camps -** Imagine kids leaving camp not only with a soccer ball and t-shirt, but with a Christian soccer resource to give them an opportunity to experience Christian growth and discovery.

- **Missionary Outreach Tool -** Because of soccer's appeal around the world, *Beyond Soccer* is an excellent way to help missionaries develop relationships, share the gospel and offer a tool for continued Christian growth.

- **International Soccer Tours**

- **Youth Soccer Tournaments**

- **Bible Studies**

- **Team Gifts**

- **Outreach Opportunities**

To find out more about the next Operation: Soccer Outreach, stay tuned to the Beyond Soccer web site – www.beyondsoccer.org.

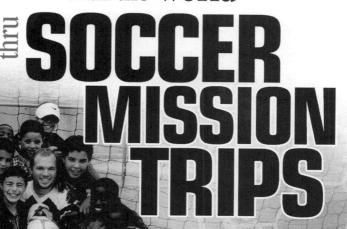

Web Site

We have developed a web site to complement the *Beyond Soccer* books. By logging on to www.beyondsoccer.org, you can:

- Sign up for our e-mail newsletter for more devotionals, special offers and updates.

- Order Beyond Soccer gear and much more from our online store.

- Send us your questions and comments.

- Find out more about Beyond Soccer ministries.

- Find links to our partner organizations and friends.

- Read more information about our guest writers and where they are now.

- E-mail us your soccer stories.

- Submit your own devotionals for consideration in future books.

- Tell a friend about Beyond Soccer.

- Join our mailing list.

- Contact us.